MISCELLANEOUS COMPOS

THE Berceuse, opus 57, published June, 1845, is the very sophistication of the art of musical ornamentation. It is built on a tonic and dominant base—the triad of the tonic and the chord of the dominant seventh. A rocking theme is set over this *basso ostinato* and the most enchanting effects are produced. The rhythm never alters in the bass, and against this background, like the monotone of a dark gray sky, the composer manipulates an astonishing variety of fireworks, florid and subdued, but all delicate in tracery and design—modulations from pigeon-egg blue to Nile green, most misty and subtle modulations that dissolve, and for a moment the sky is peppered with tiny double stars each independently tinted. Within a small segment of the chromatic bow Chopin has caught and imprisoned new, fantastically dissonant colors. It is all a miracle. And after the drawn-out chord of the dominant seventh and the rain of silvery fire ceases we then realize that the piece is a delicious illusion, an ululation in the key of D flat, the apotheosis of pyrotechnical *colorature*. Niecks quotes Alexandre Dumas *fils*, who calls the Berceuse "muted music," but introduces a Turkish bath comparison which quite crushes the sentiment. As for the cradle and the child I never could conjure up either, despite the rhythm. Chopin was a hopeless bachelor and, like Charles Lamb, had not much affection for other people's children. For me the Berceuse is an exercise in transcendental tone-spinning.

The Barcarolle, opus 60, was published in September, 1846, and is another highly elaborated work. One day Tausig, the great piano virtuoso, promised De Lenz to play him the Barcarolle, adding: "That is a performance that must not be undertaken before more than two persons. I shall play you my own self. I love the piece, but take it up rarely." De Lenz got the music, but it did not please him; it seemed a long movement in the nocturne style, a Babel of figuration on a lightly laid foundation. But he found that he had made a mistake; and hearing it played by Tausig, confessed that the *virtuoso* had infused into the nine pages of enervating music, of one and the same long-breathed rhythm, so much interest, so much action, so much motion, that he regretted the long piece was no longer. Tausig's conception of the Barcarolle was this: "There are two persons concerned in the affair; it is a love affair in a *discrète* gondola; let us say this *mise en scène* is the symbol of a lovers' meeting generally. This is expressed in thirds and sixths; the dualism of two notes—persons—is maintained

throughout; all is t   his modulation in C sh..   lce *sfogato*—there are kiss and embrace. This is evident. When, after three bars of introduction, the theme, lightly rocking in the bass solo, enters in the fourth, this theme is nevertheless made use of throughout the whole fabric only as an accompaniment, and on this the *cantilena* in two parts is laid; we have thus a continuous tender dialogue." The Barcarolle is a Nocturne painted on a large canvas. Italianate in color at times—Schumann has said that melodically Chopin occasionally leans over Germany into Italy—it pulsates with sentiment. It sounds like a lament for the vanished splendors of Venice, the Queen of the Adriatic. In bars 8, 9 and 10, counting backward, Louis Ehlert finds obscurities in the middle voices; but for twentieth century ears they are so many color notes for the composer's musical palette.

The Bolero, opus 19, has a Polacca-like flavor; there is but little Spanish in its ingredients. It is merely a memorandum of Chopin's early essays in dance-forms. It was published in 1834, some years before the visit to Spain. That it can be made effective in concert performance has been often proved. It is for fleet-fingered pianists, and the principal theme has a Polish rhythmical ring, though Iberian in character. It is in the key of A minor, its *coda* in A major. The Tarentelle is in A flat major, and is numbered opus 43. It was published in 1841 and bears no dedication. Composed at Nohant, it is as little Italian as the Bolero is Spanish. Chopin's visit to Italy was of too short a duration to affect him, at least in the dance style. He found the familiar rhythm ready-made, but imparted little of its whirling madness to its measures. His Tarentelle is without the Neapolitan tang and hardly ranks with the examples of Heller or Liszt or Thalberg. One finds in Chopin's effort little of the frenzy ascribed to it in the review by Schumann. But it is graceful, and for the amateur pianist a "grateful" piece.

The Allegro de Concert, in A major, opus 46, was published in November, 1841. It has all the superficial characteristics of a concerto, and may be a truncated one—much more so, for instance, than Schumann's F minor Sonata, called "Concert sans Orchestre." There are seemingly *tutti* in this Chopin composition, the solo not beginning until the eighty-seventh bar. But it must not be supposed that these long introductory passages are ineffective. On the contrary, the Allegro is one of Chopin's most difficult works; it abounds in risky skips, ambuscades of dangerous double-notes. The principal themes are both bold and expressive. The general structure and brilliant coloring strikingly adapt the piece to concert performance, and perhaps Schumann was correct in believing that Chopin had originally sketched it for piano and orchestra. Maybe this is the fragment of a concerto for two pianos, which Chopin, in a letter written at Vienna, December 21, 1830, said he would play in public with his friend Nidecki if he succeeded in fashioning it to his satisfaction. And is there any significance in the fact that Chopin, when sending the manuscript to Fontana—probably in the Summer of 1841—calls it a concerto? While the Allegro de Concert has not greatly added to Chopin's reputation, nevertheless it contains the germs of a powerful composition. It is virile, to say the least. Jean Louis Nicodé gave it an orchestral garb, after arranging it for two pianos. The original version is preferable, if for nothing else because the Dresden composer inserted a working-out section of more than seventy bars, certainly an unjustifiable proceeding, not to be compared with Tausig's tactful editing of the E minor Concerto.

Chopin varied a rondo from Halévy's "Ludovic" entitled "Je vends des scapulaires," and it appeared as his opus 12. In 1883 it was published, and is in B flat major. It is Chopin and water; Gallic *eau sucrée* at that. The piece is tastefully written, is not difficult, but is artificial. In May, 1851, appeared the posthumous Variations in E major on a German air and without opus number. Evidently composed before Chopin's opus 1 (1824?), they are musically tenuous, though written by one who knew the resources of the keyboard. In 1830 this composition was already in the hands of Haslinger, the publisher. The last Variation, a Waltz, is the brightest of the set. The Funeral March in C minor, opus 72, No. 2, composed in 1829, recalls Mendelssohn; the trio has the processional quality of a Parisian funeral cortège. The piece is of modest proportions and is in nowise remarkable. The three Écossaises, posthumously published in 1830 as opus 72, are in D, G, and D flat major, respectively, and are little dances, Schottisches, and nothing more. No. 2, before the present mania for eccentric steps, was a much liked and graceful dance. Slight in texture as are several of the above named compositions, they must be critically considered and included in any comprehensive edition of Chopin's music.

James Huneker

Thematic Index.

Berceuse.
Andante. Op. 57.
Db major. Page. 3

Barcarolle.
Allegretto. Op. 60.
F# major. Page 9

Bolero.
Introduction. Allegro molto.
C major.

Allegro vivace. Op. 19.
Page. 21

Tarentelle.
Presto. Op. 43. Page.
Ab major. 37

Allegro de Concert.
Allegro maestoso. Op. 46.
A major. Page. 48

Variations brillantes.
Introduction. Allegro maestoso.
Bb major.

Thème. (Ronde de Ludovic.)
Allegro moderato. Op. 12.
Page. 70

Variations sur un air allemand.
(Posthumous.)
Introduction. A capriccio.
E major.

Thème. Andantino.
Page. 86

Marche funèbre.
(Posthumous.)
Tempo di Marcia. Op. 72, No 2. Page.
C minor. 96

Trois Ecossaises. (No 1.)
(Posthumous.)
Vivace. Op. 72, No 3. Page.
D major. 100

Trois Ecossaises. (No 2.)
(Posthumous.) Op. 72, No 4.
G major. Page. 101

Trois Ecossaises. (No 3.)
(Posthumous.) Op. 72, No 5.
Db major. Page. 102

à Mlle Élise Gavard

Berceuse

Revised and fingered by
Rafael Joseffy

F. Chopin. Op. 57

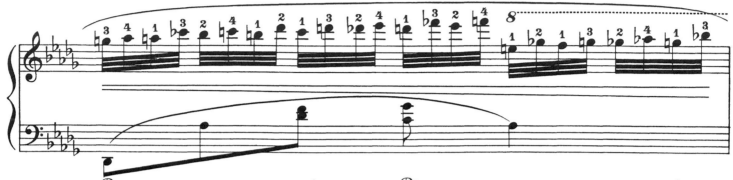

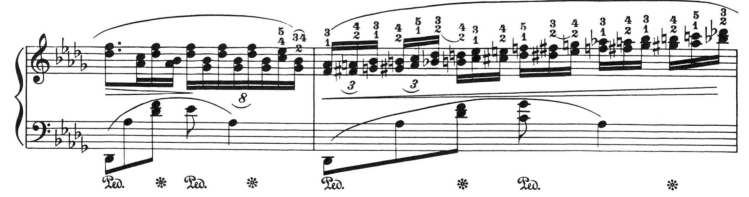

pp e leggiero sempre

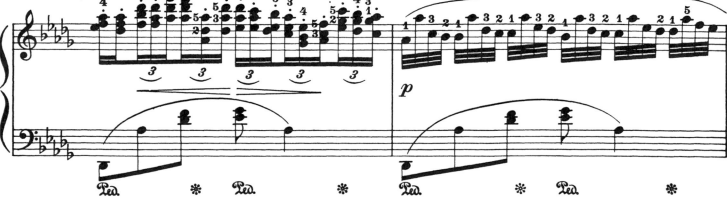

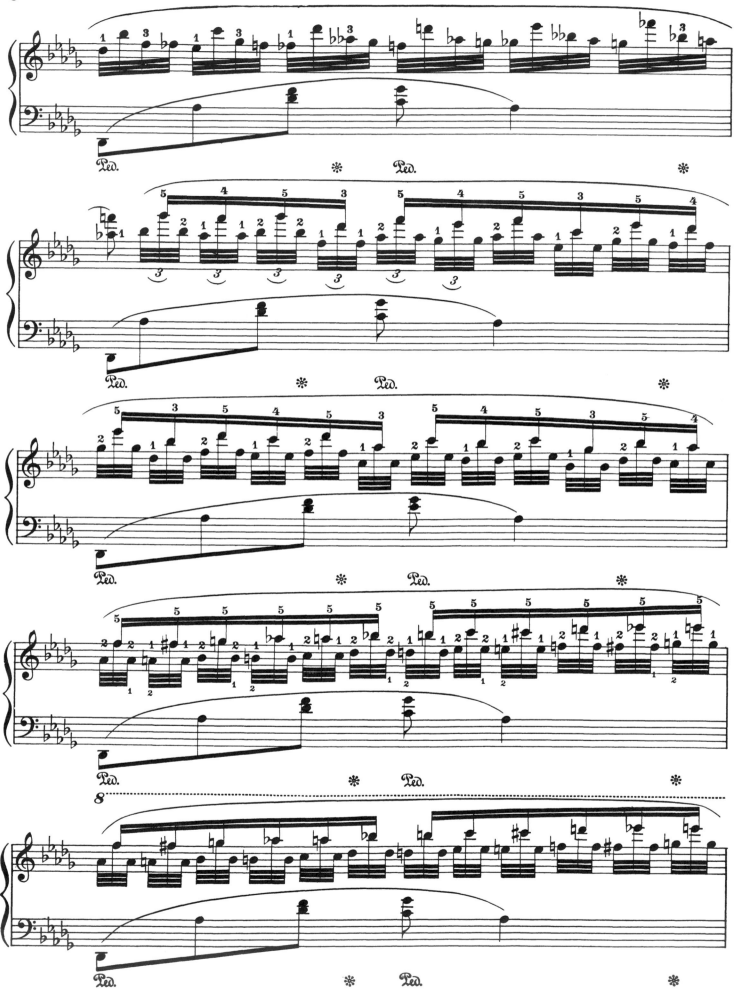

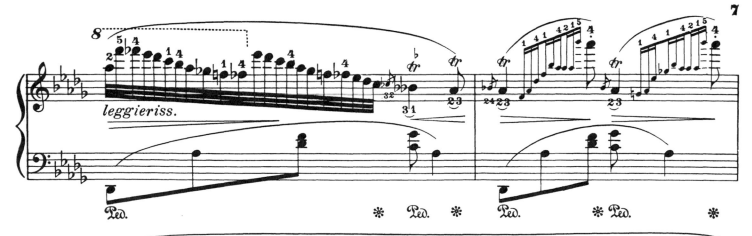

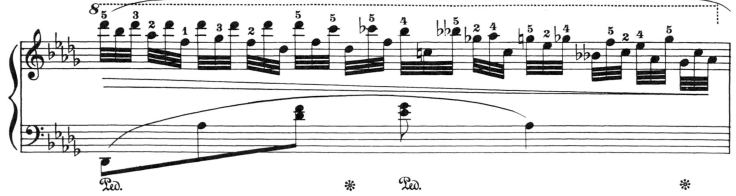

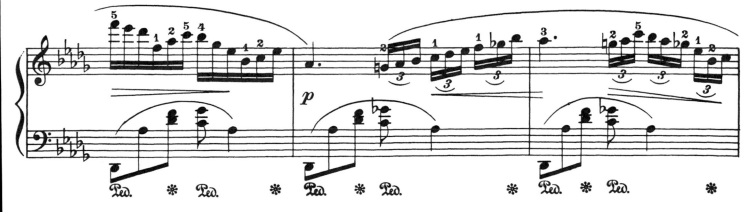

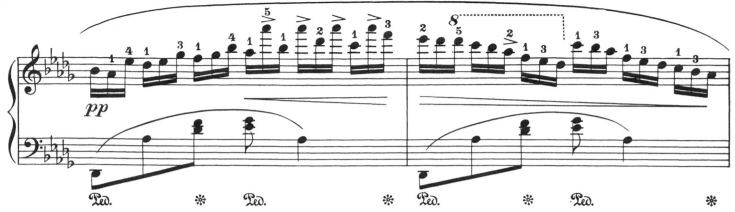

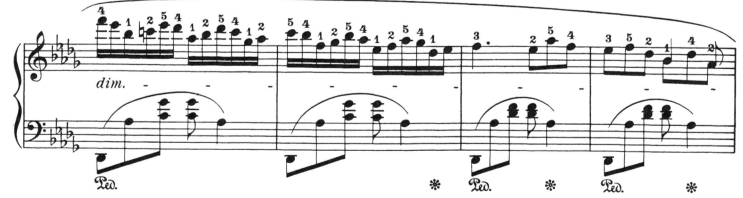

à Mᵐᵉ la Baronne de Stockhausen

Barcarolle

Revised and fingered by
Rafael Joseffy

F. Chopin. Op. 60

Ossia:

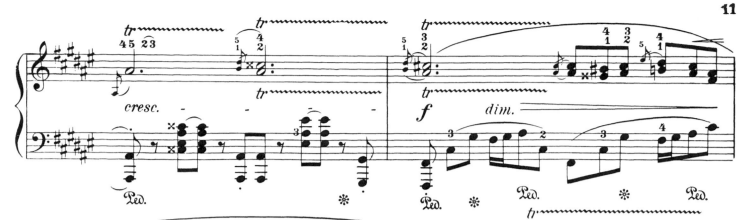

12

* In some editions:
In manchen Ausgaben:

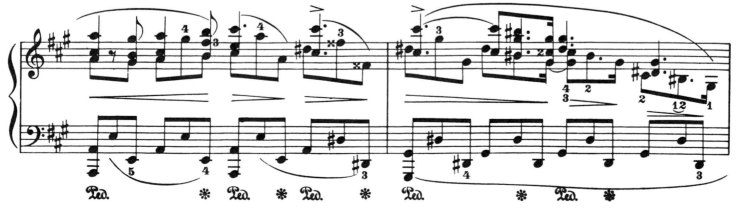

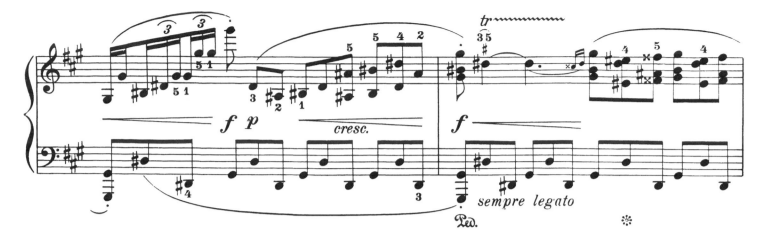

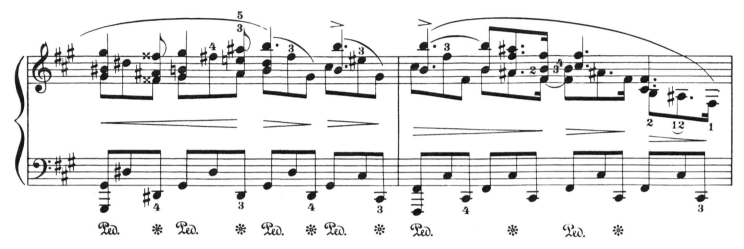

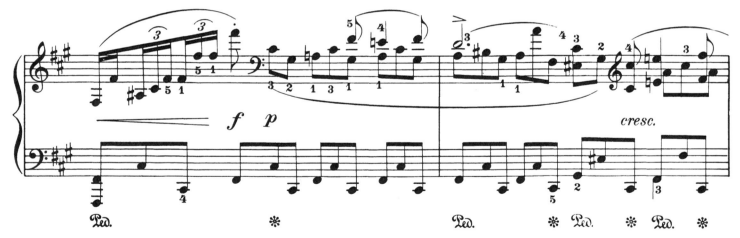

poco più mosso

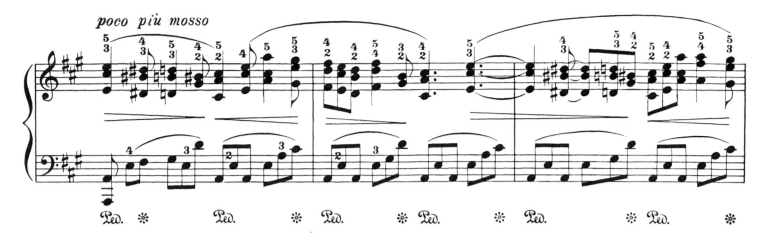

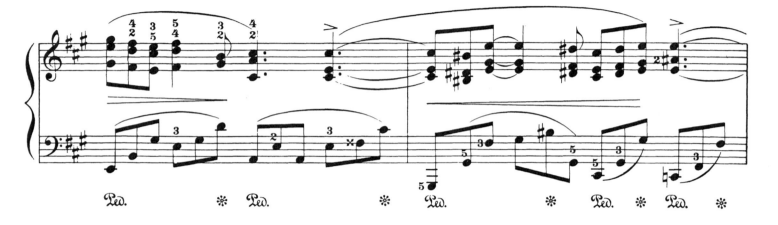

Meno mosso

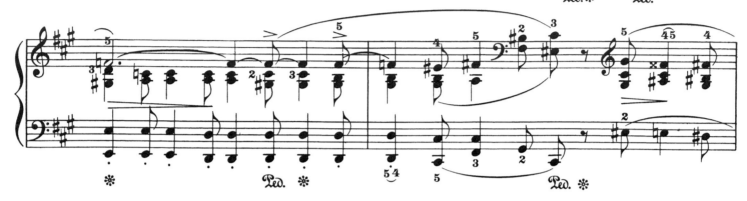

Tempo I°

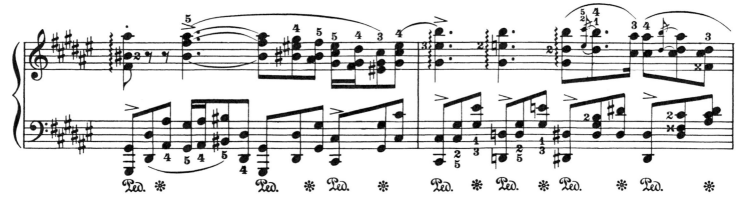

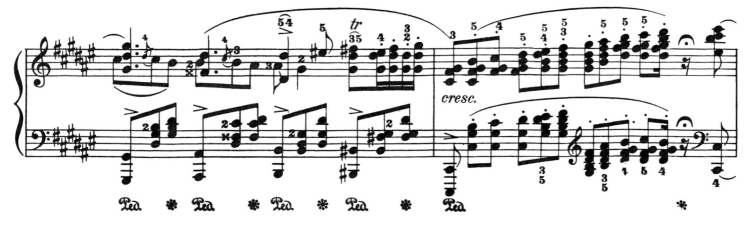

Più mosso

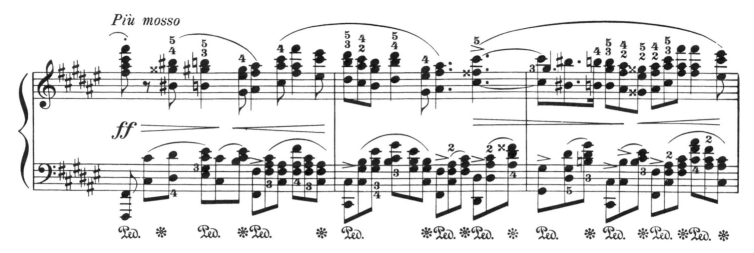

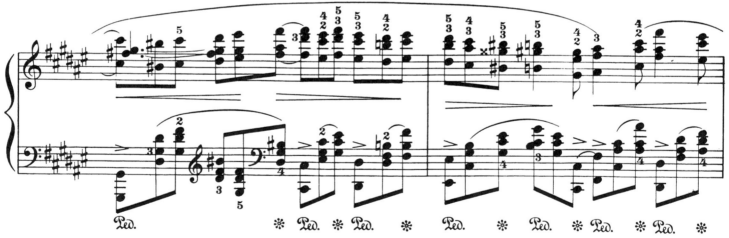

Tempo I°

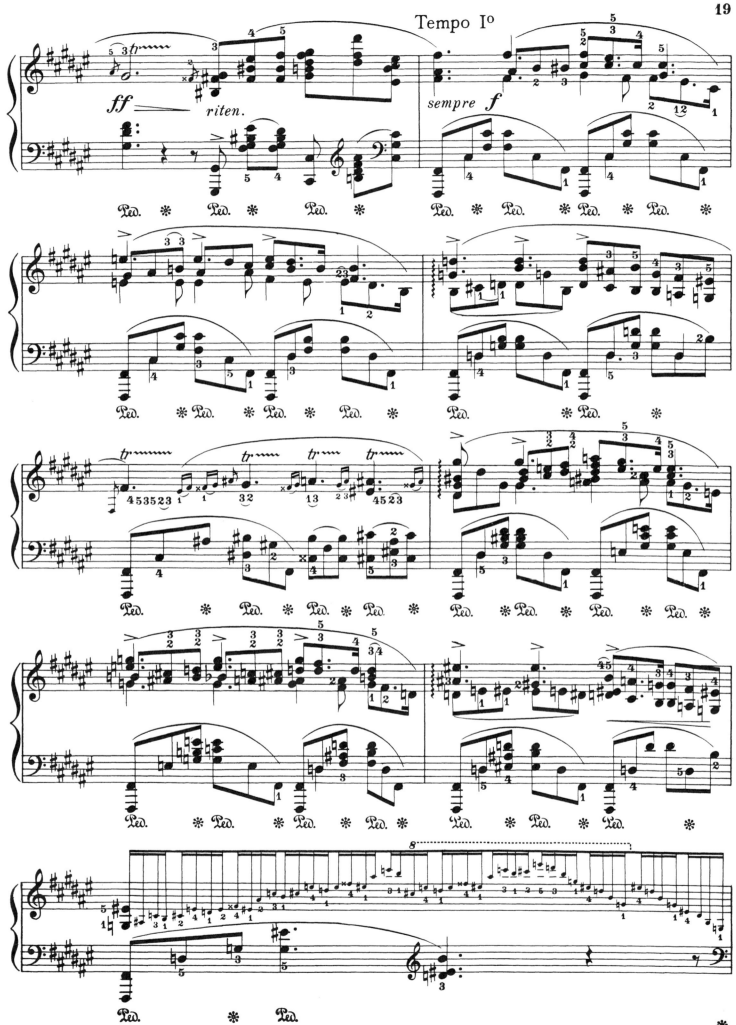

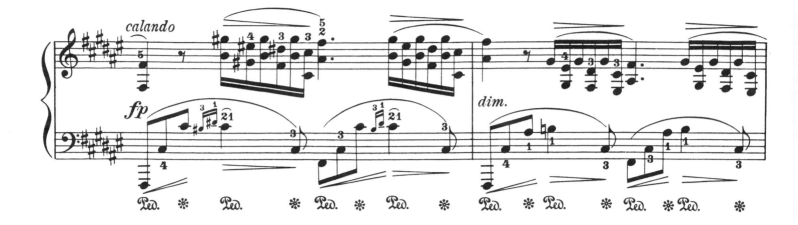

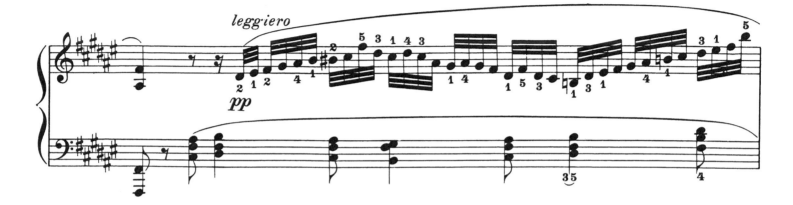

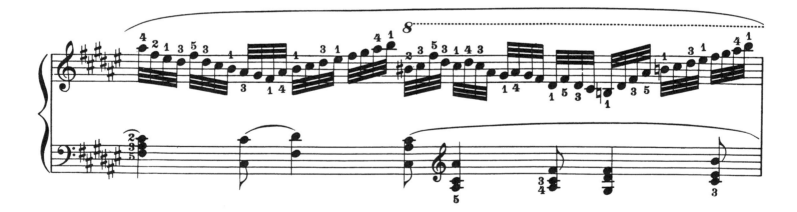

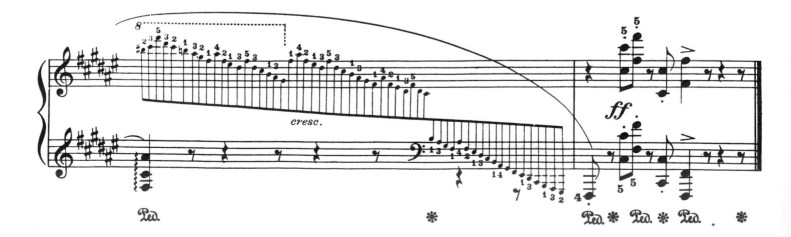

a Mme la Comtesse E. de Flahault

Bolero

Revised and fingered by
Rafael Joseffy

F. Chopin. Op. 19

Introduzione
Molto allegro (♩. = 88)

Più lento (♪ = 104)
con anima

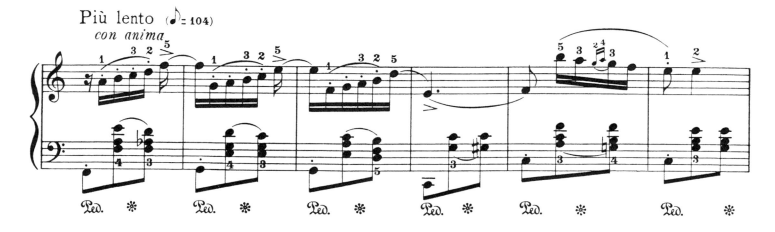

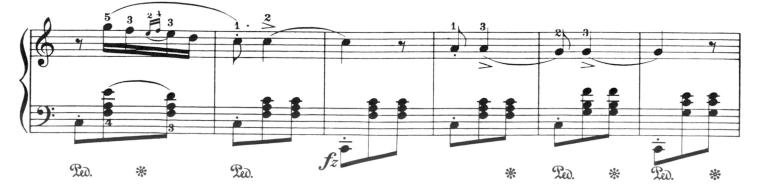

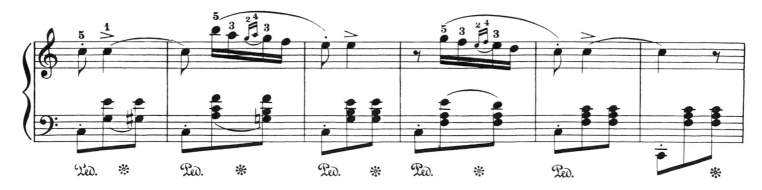

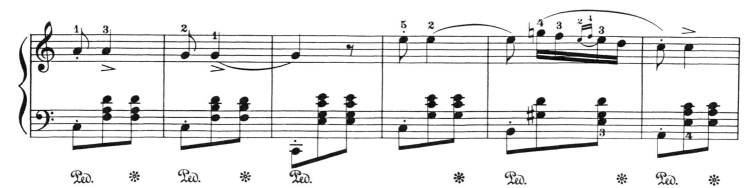

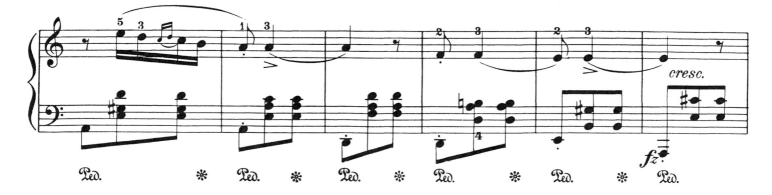

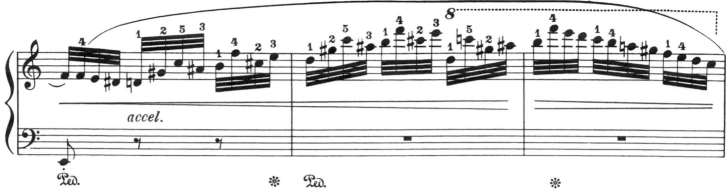

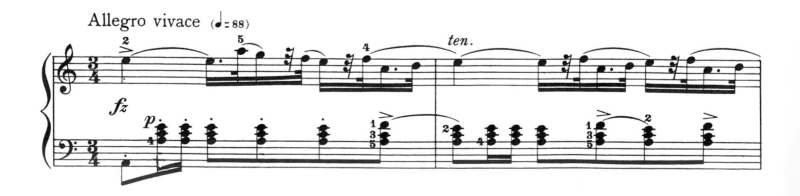

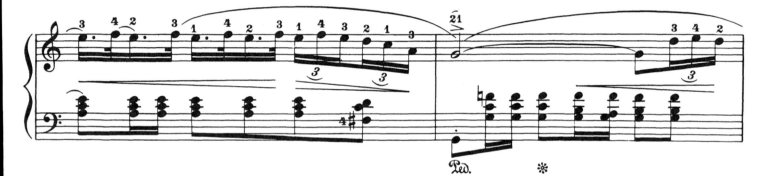

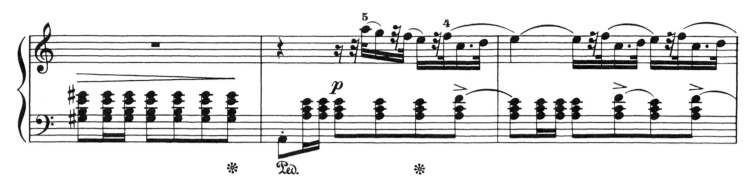

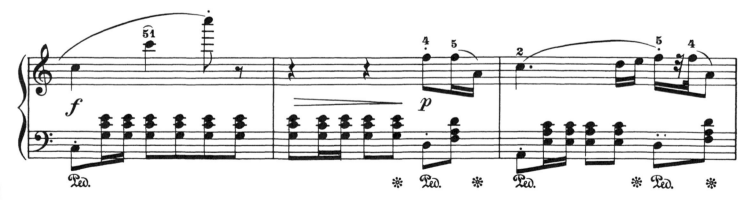

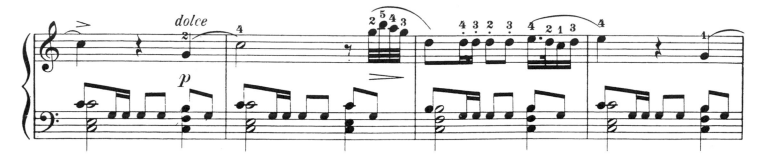

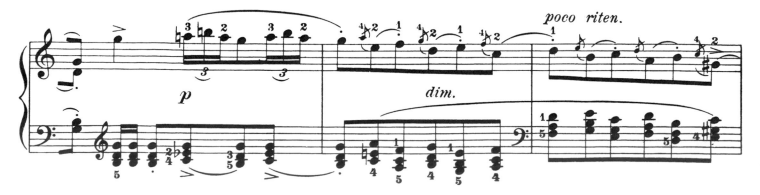

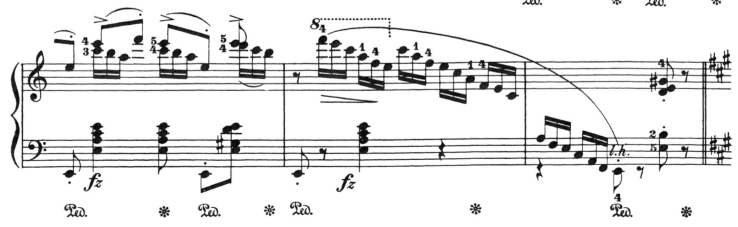

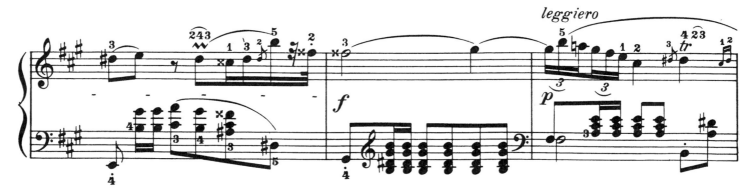

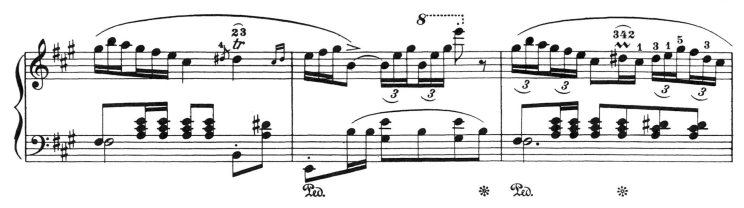

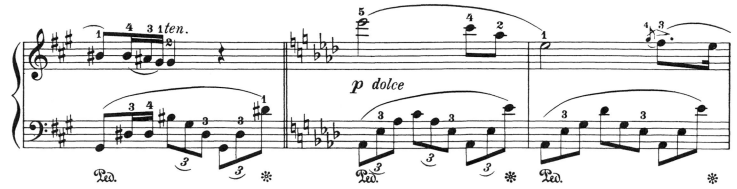

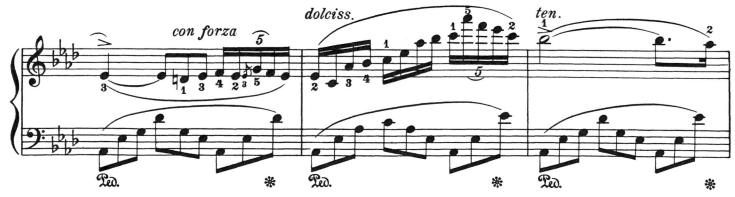

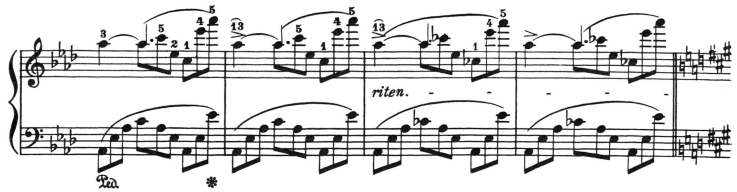

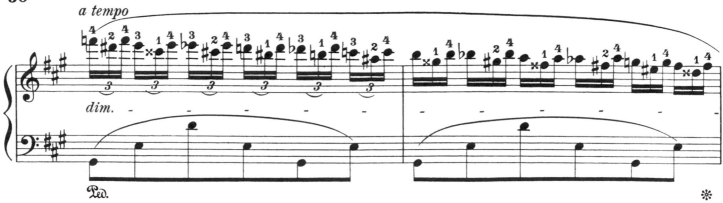

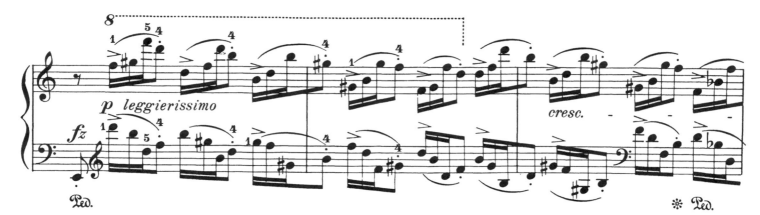

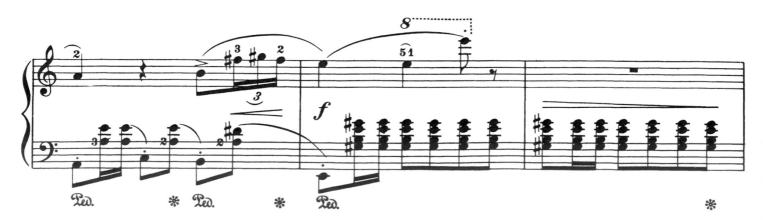

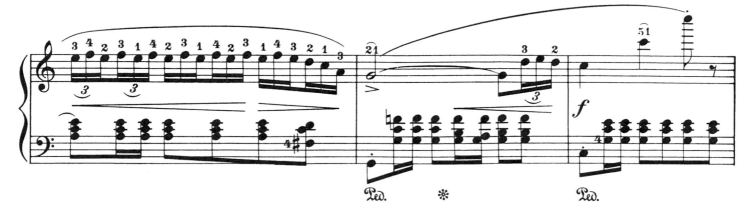

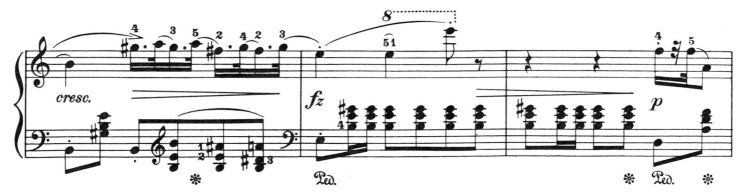

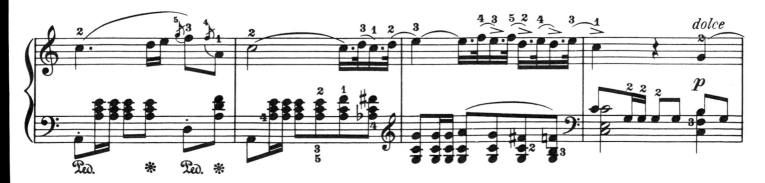

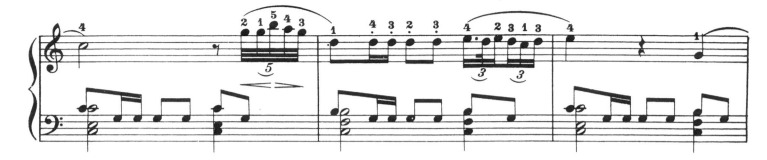

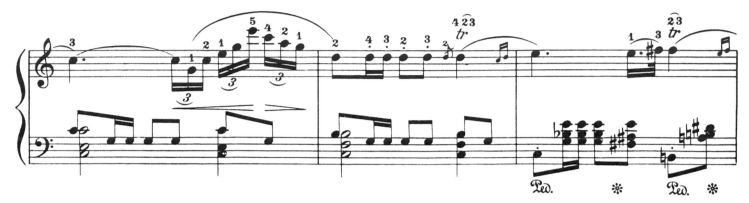

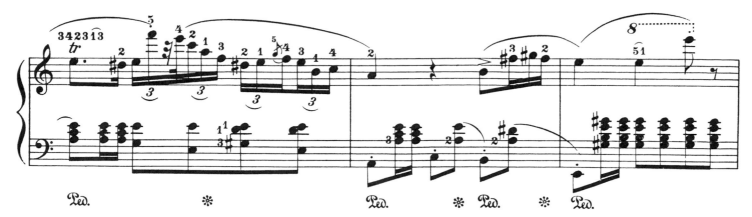

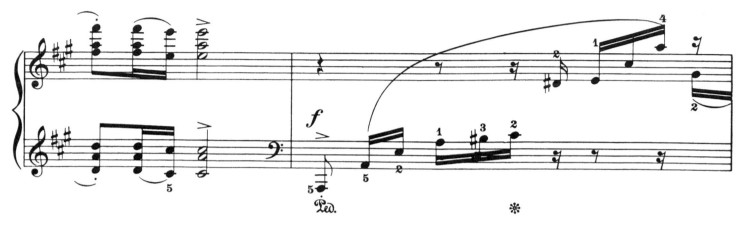

Tarentelle

Revised and fingered by
Rafael Joseffy

F. Chopin. Op. 43

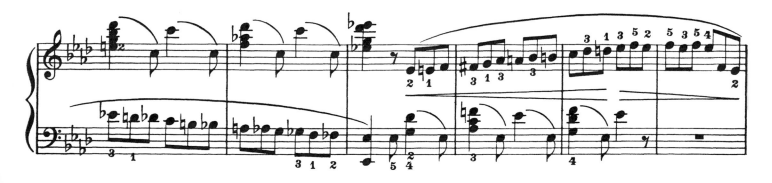

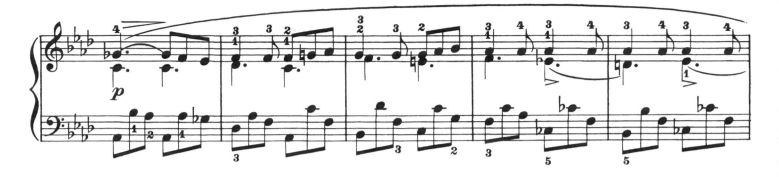

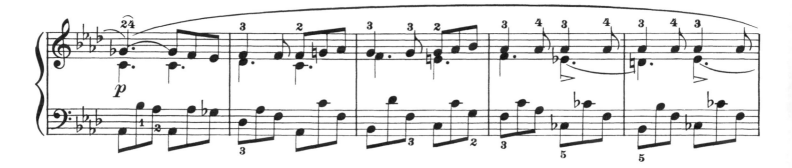

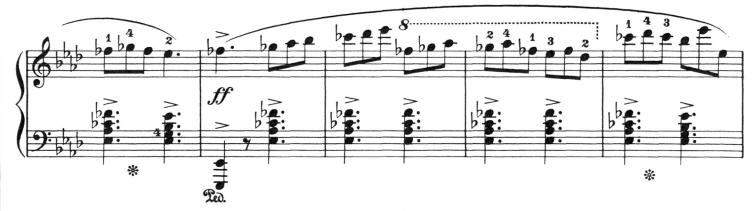

Più animato

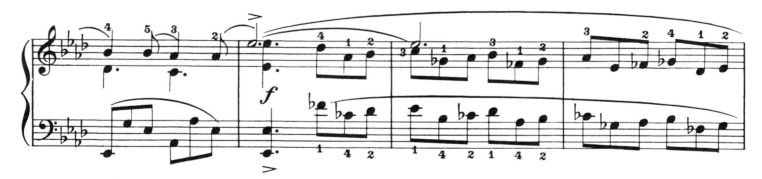

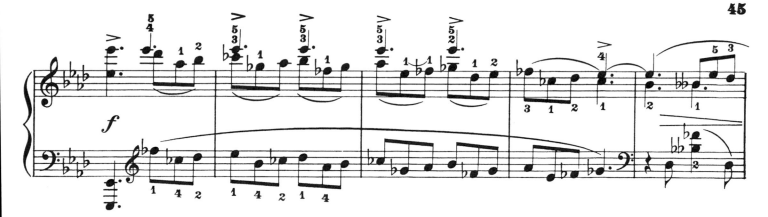

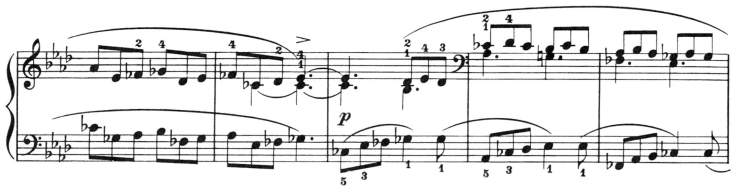

pp sempre più animato e poco a poco cresc.

cresc.

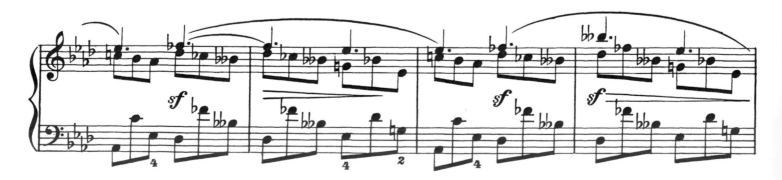

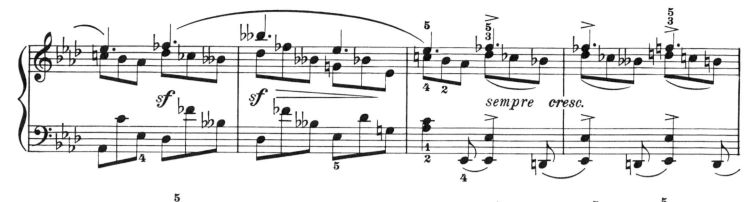

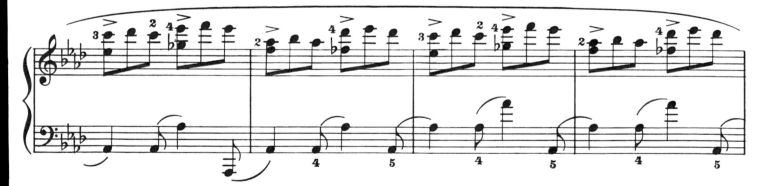

a M.lle F. Müller

Allegro de Concert

Revised and fingered by
Rafael Joseffy

F. Chopin. Op. 46

Allegro maestoso

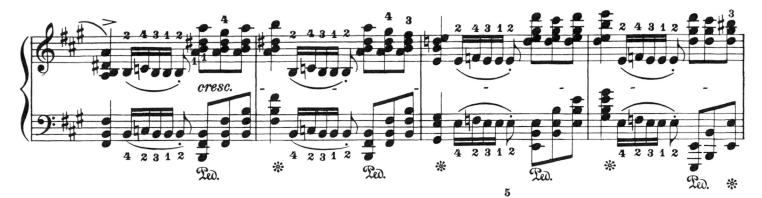

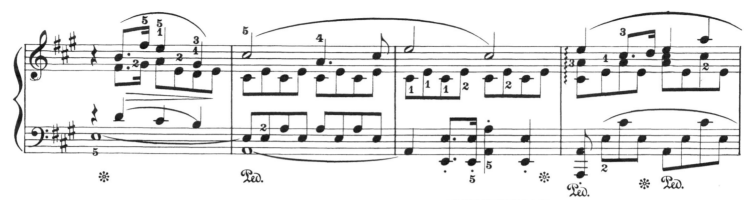

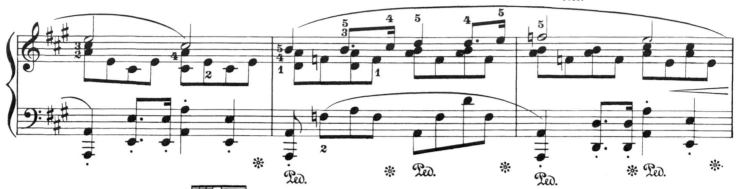

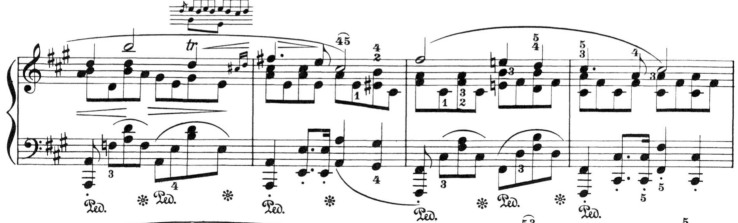

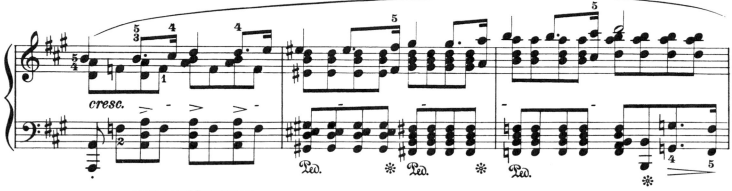

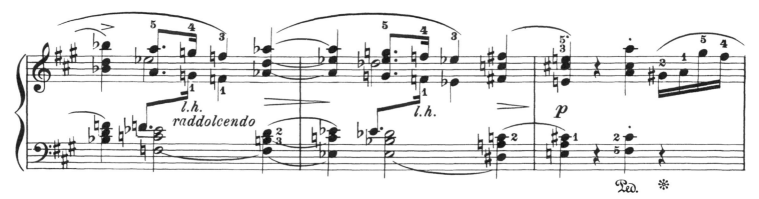

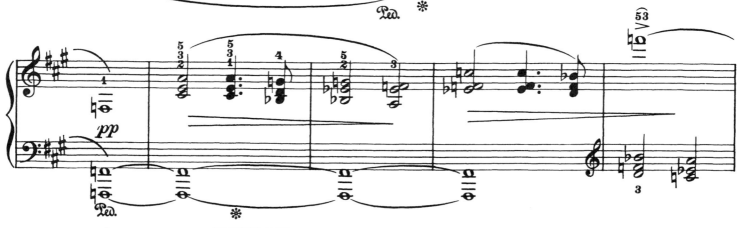

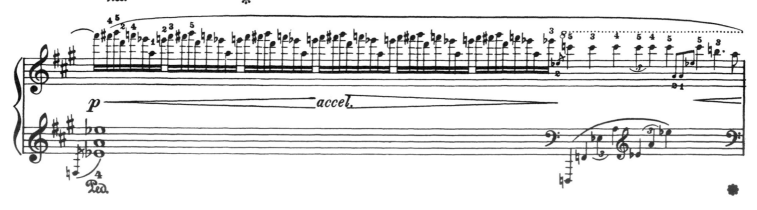

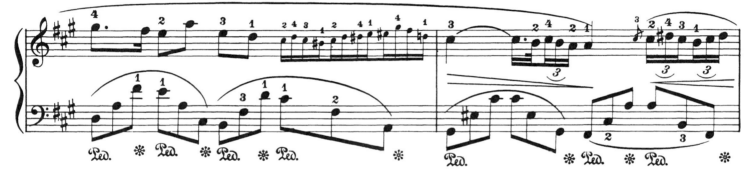

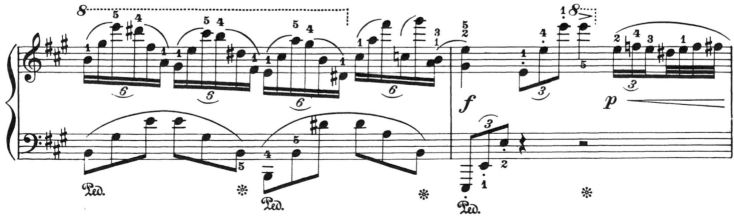

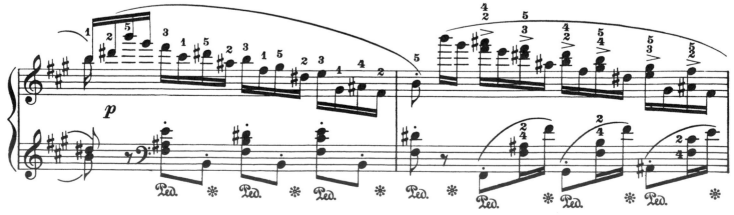

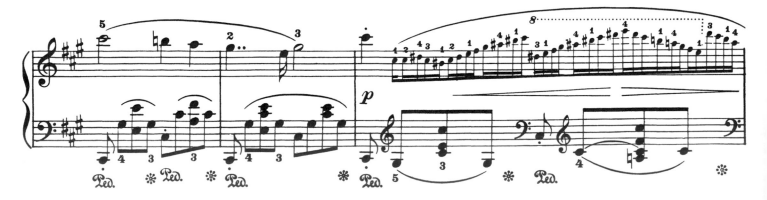

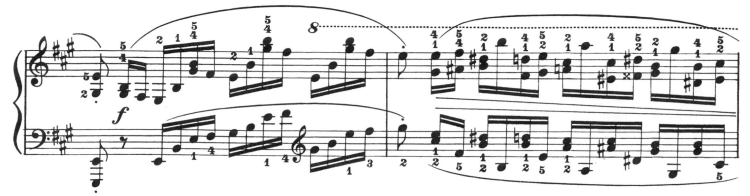

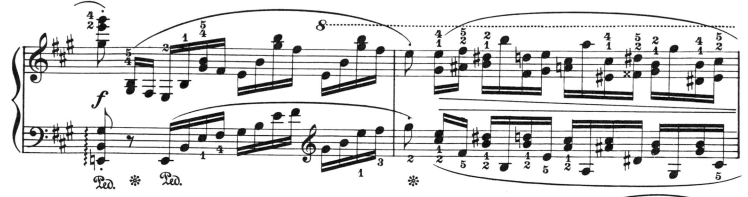

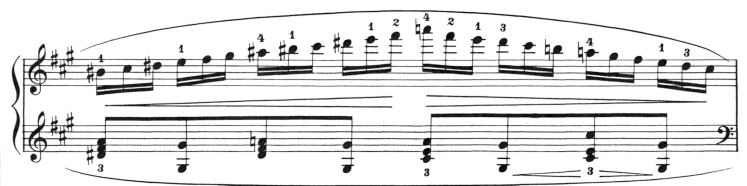

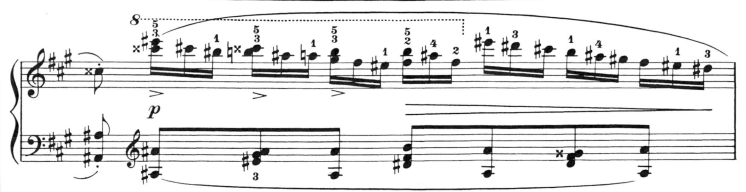

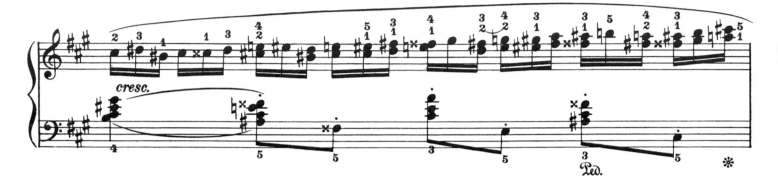

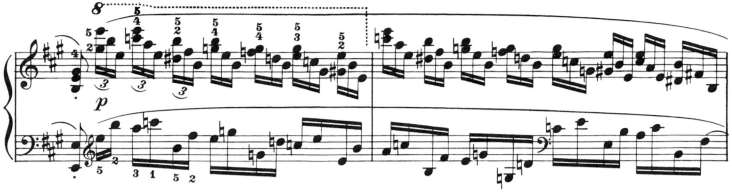

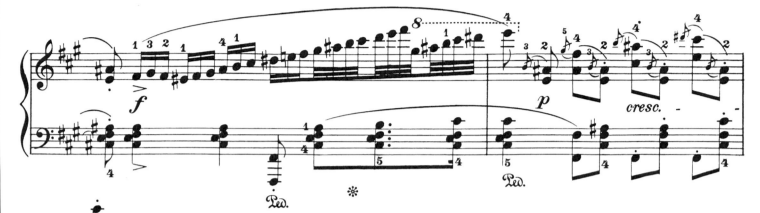

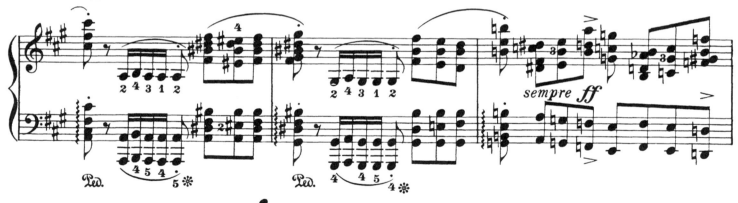

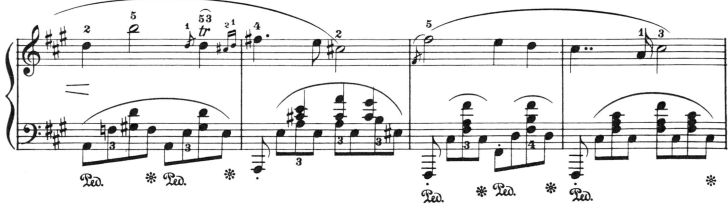

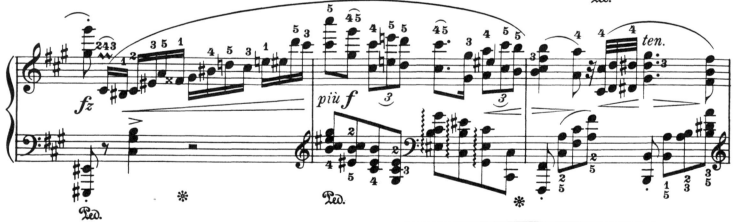

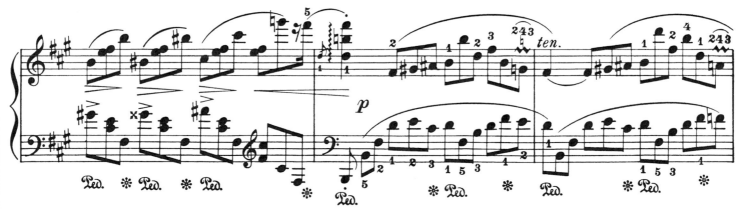

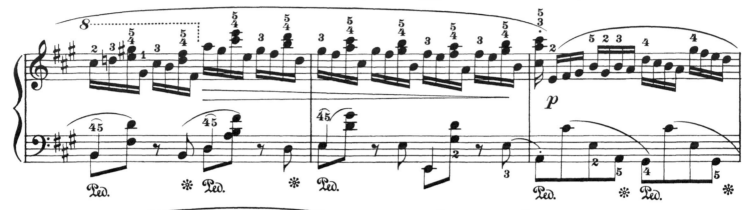

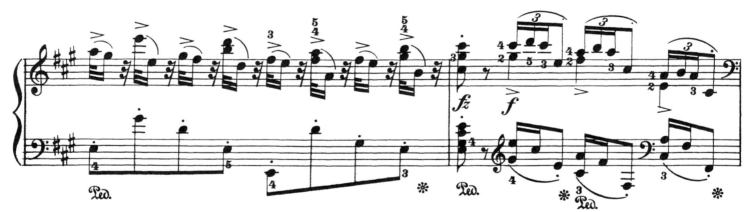

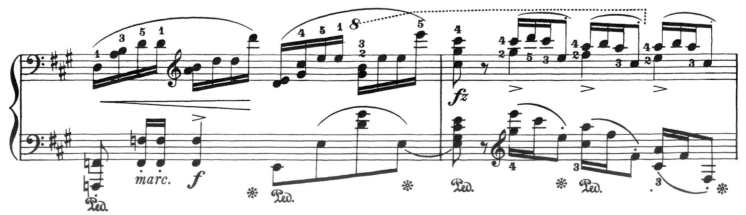

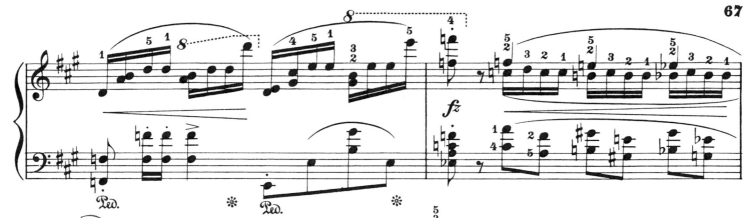

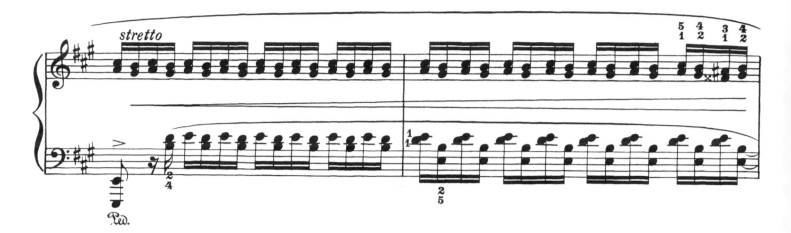

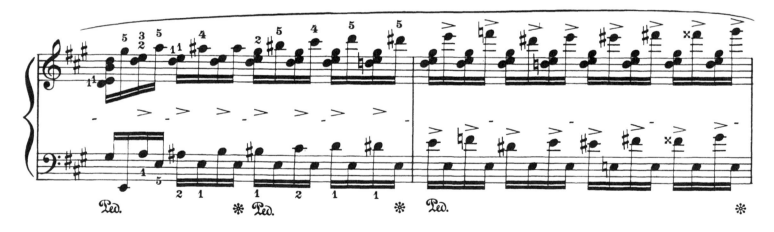

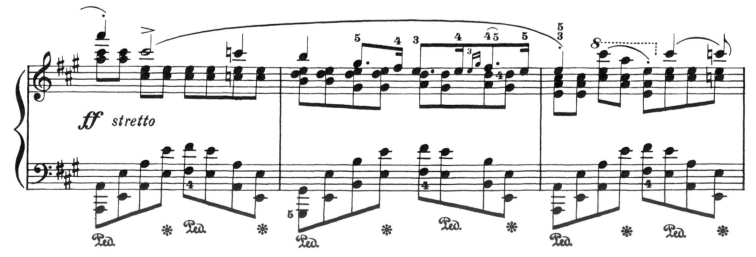

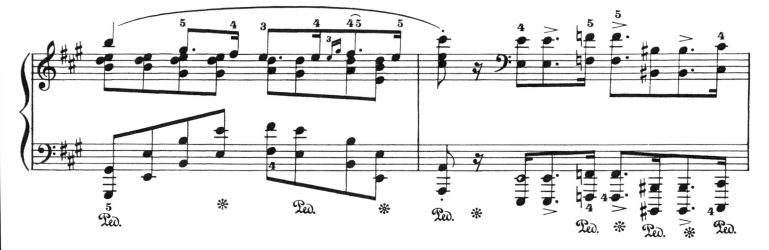

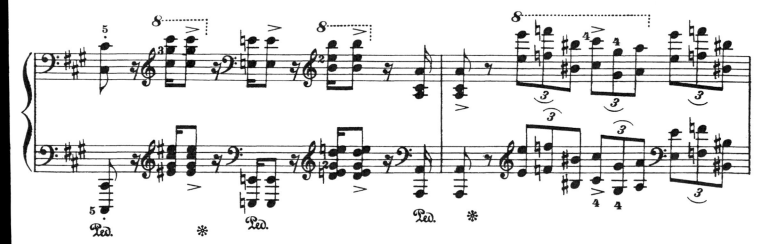

A Mme Emma Horsford

Variations brillantes

(Sur le Rondeau favori: «Je vends des scapulaires,» de Ludovic)

Revised and fingered by
Rafael Joseffy

F. Chopin. Op. 12

Introduction
Allegro maestoso (♩ = 118)

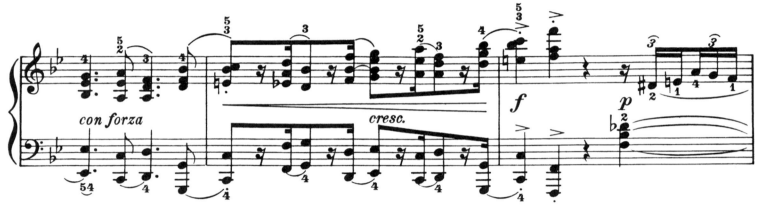

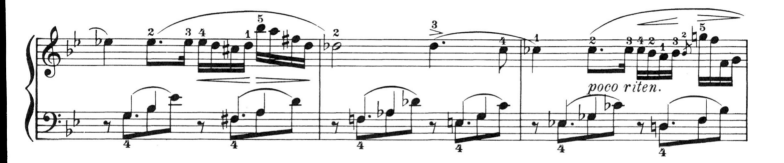

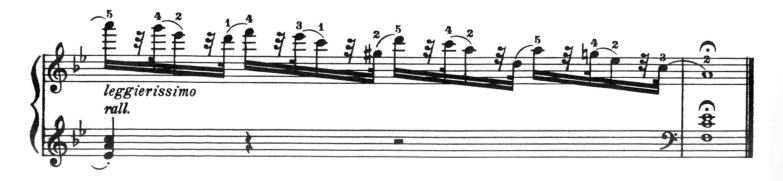

Thème
Allegro moderato

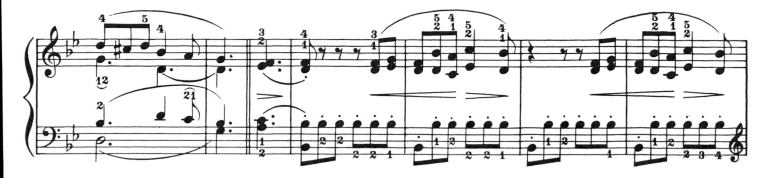

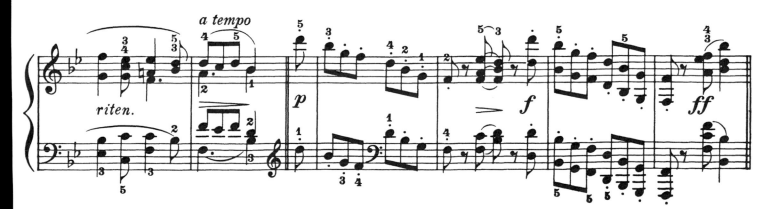

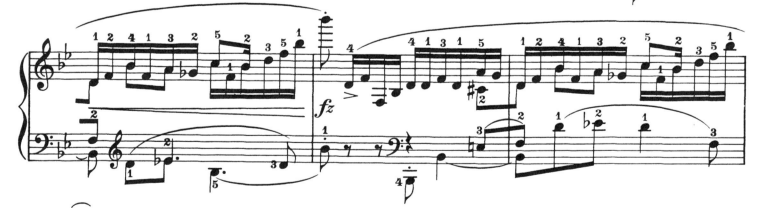

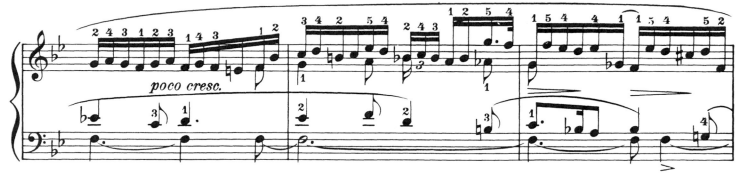

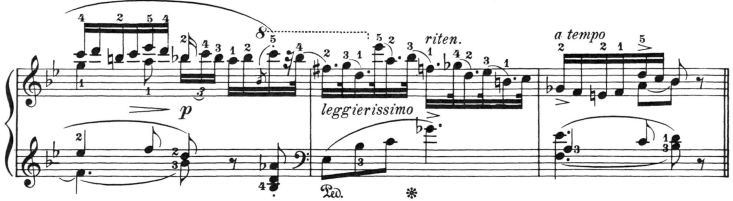

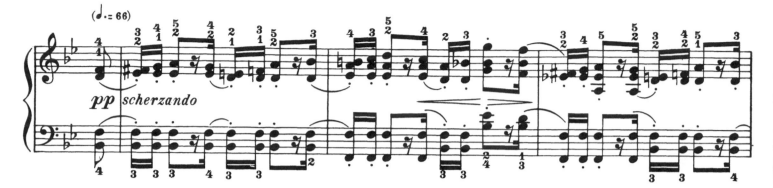

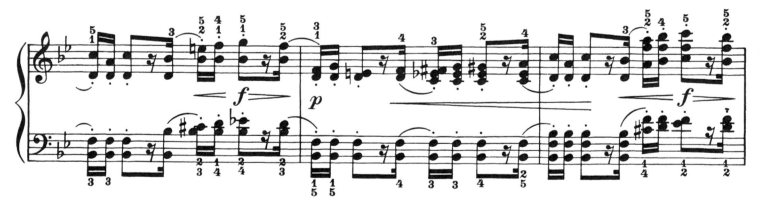

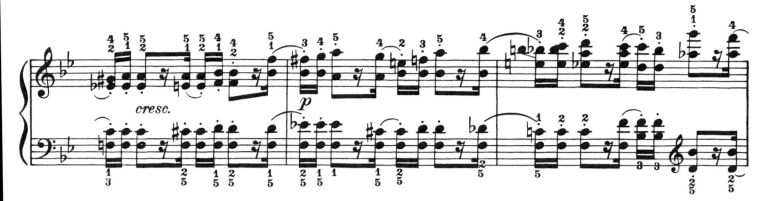

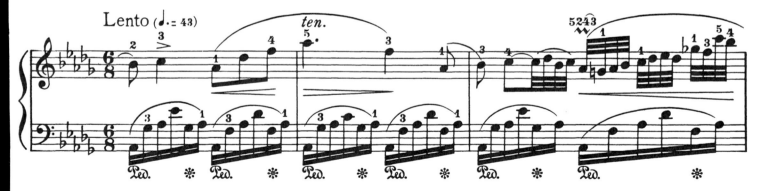

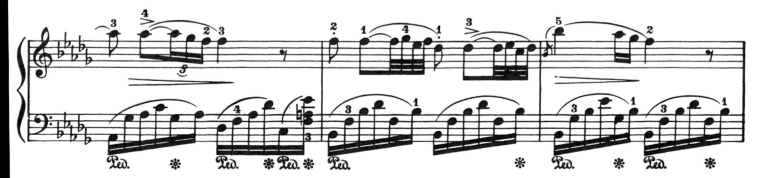

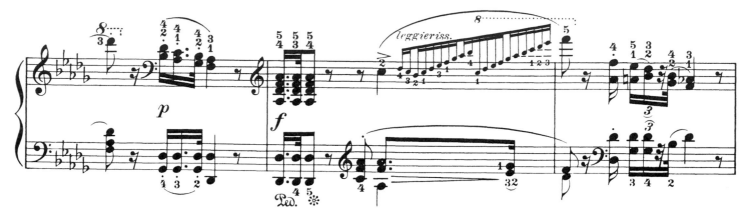

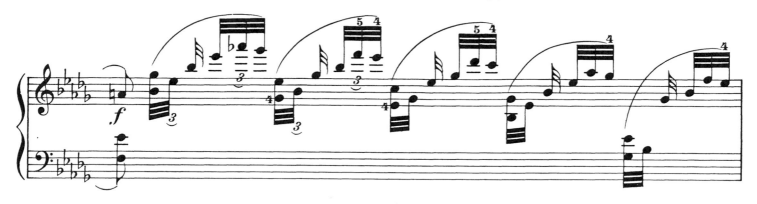

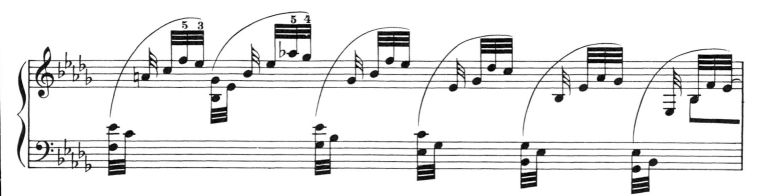

Scherzo vivace (♩.= 88)

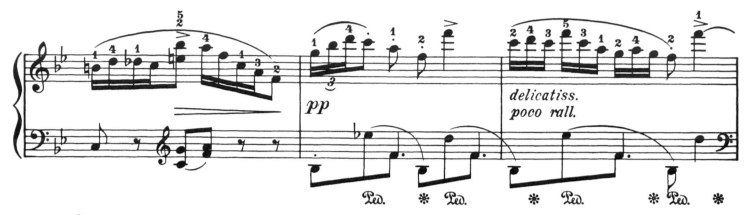

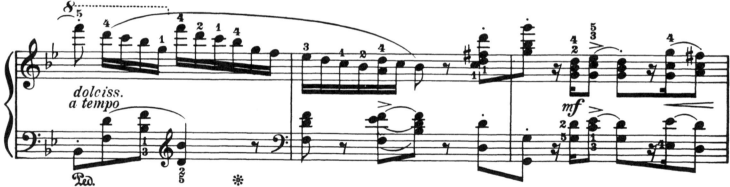

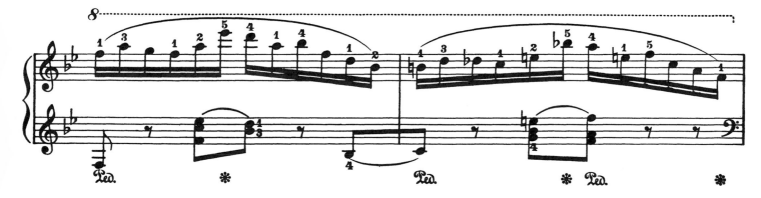

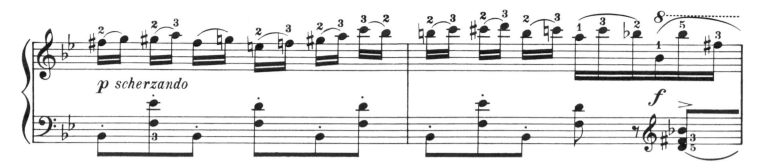

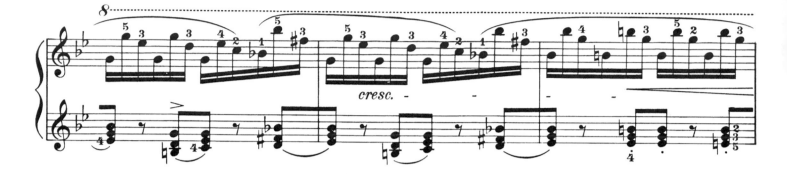

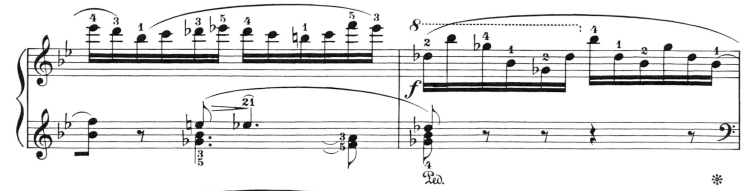

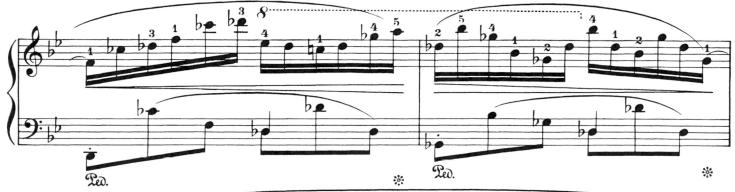

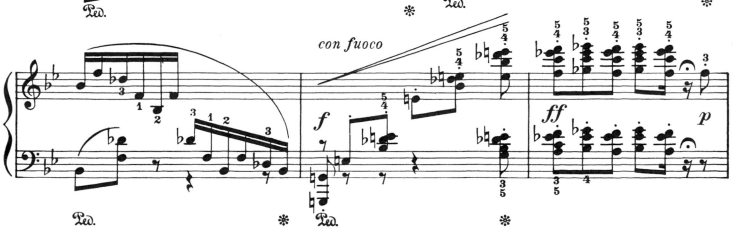

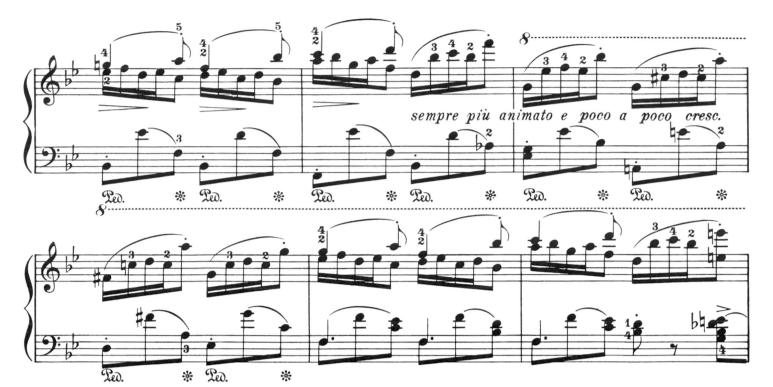

sempre più animato e poco a poco cresc.

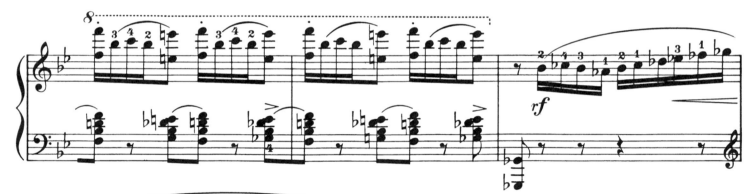

rf

cresc.

ff

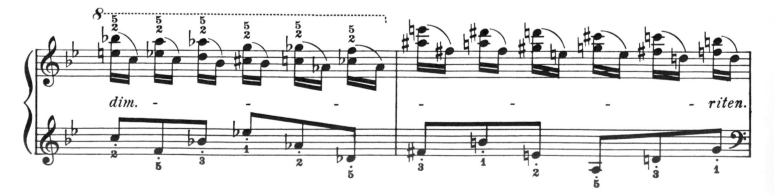

dim. -   *-*   *-*   *-*   *-*   *-*   *- riten.*

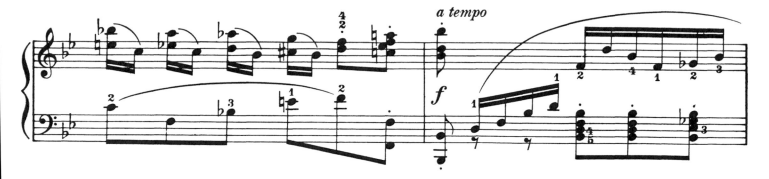

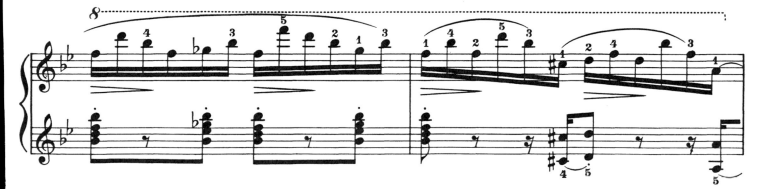

Variations

(Sur un Air national-allemand)
(Œuvre posthume)

Revised and fingered by
Rafael Joseffy

F. Chopin

Introduction
A capriccio

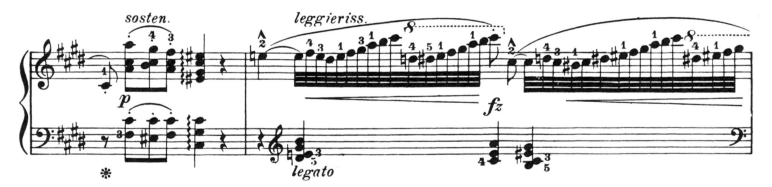

sempre legato

a tempo

pp e poco rall.

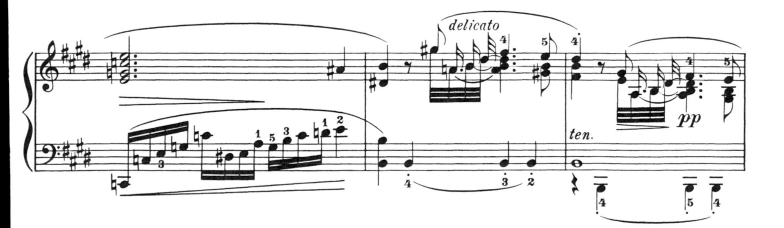

delicato

ten.

pp

p

dim. e rall.

Thème
Andantino (♩ = 54)
semplice senza ornamenti

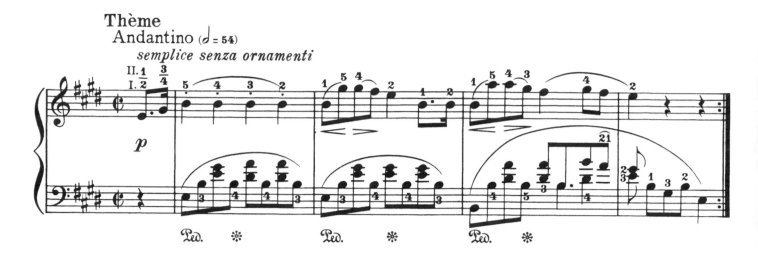

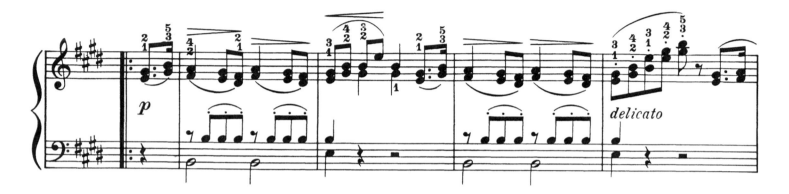

Var. I
Elegantamente (♩ = 80)

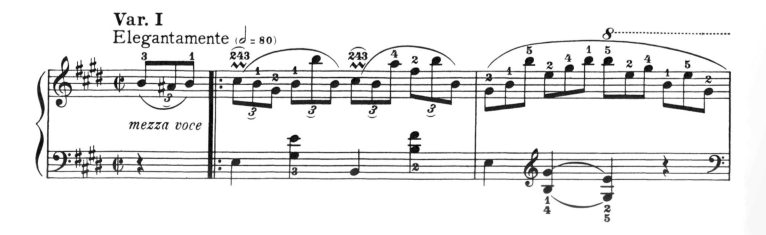

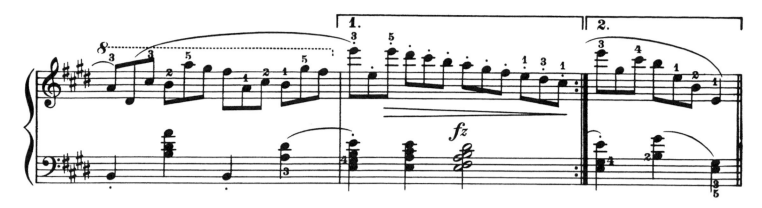

Var. II
Scherzando

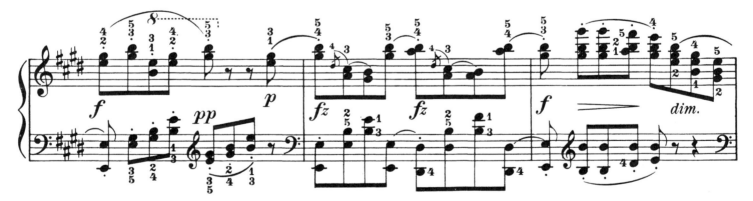

Var. III
Tranquillamente (♩ = 60)

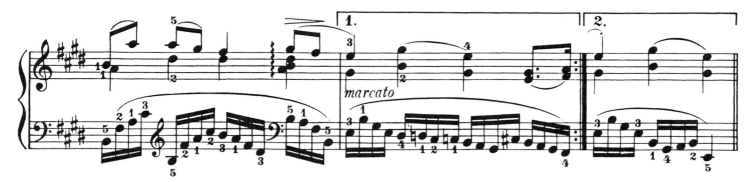

Var. IV

Meno mosso (♩ = 63)

Tempo di Valse (♩. = 72)

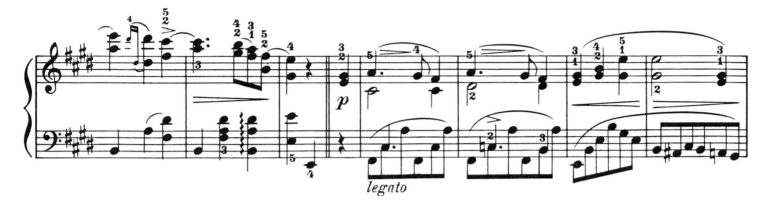

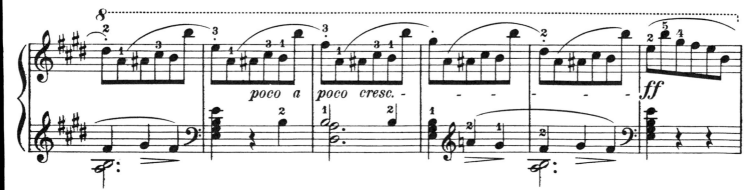

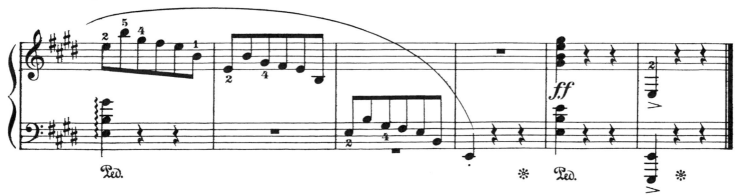

Marche funèbre
(Œuvre posthume)

Revised and fingered by
Rafael Joseffy

F. Chopin. Op. 72, No. 2
(1829)

Tempo di Marcia (♩ = 84)

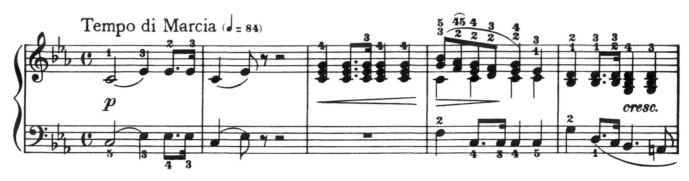

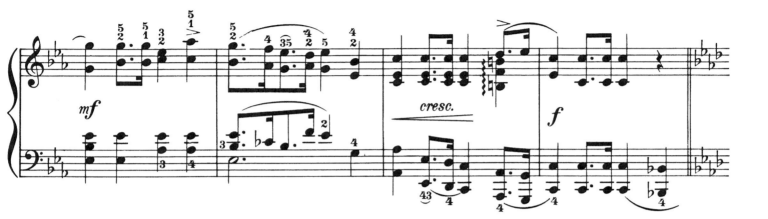

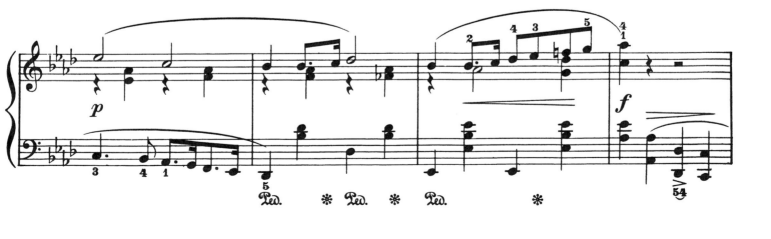

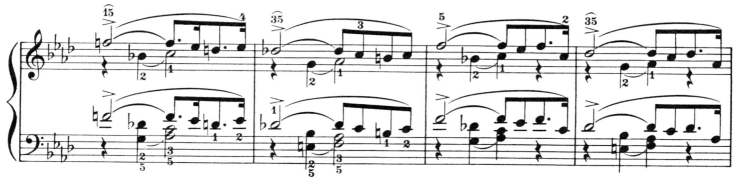

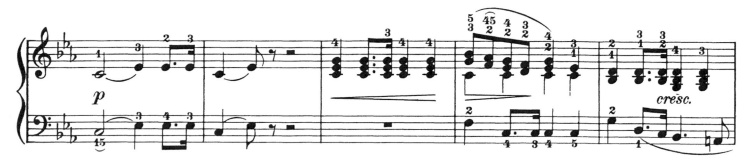

Trois Écossaises

(Œuvre posthume)

Revised and fingered by
Rafael Joseffy

F. Chopin. Op. 72, No. 3
(1830)

1.

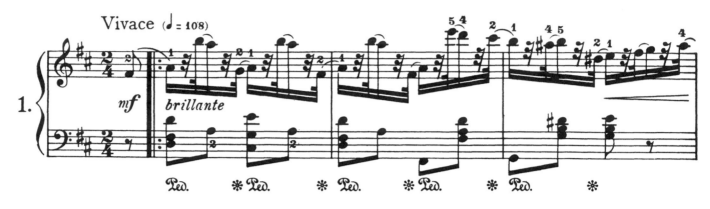

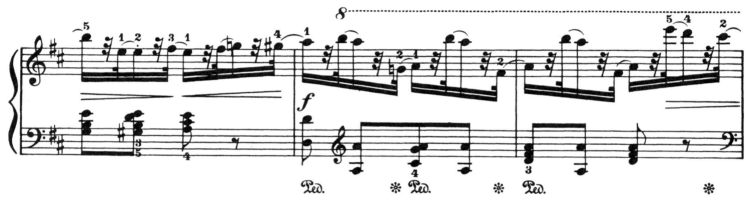

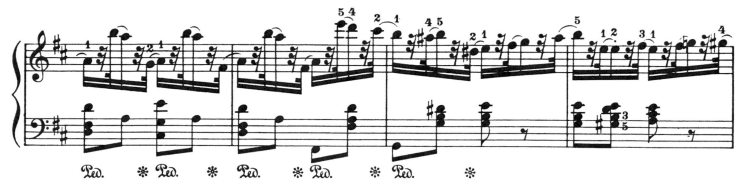

F. Chopin. Op. 72, No. 4

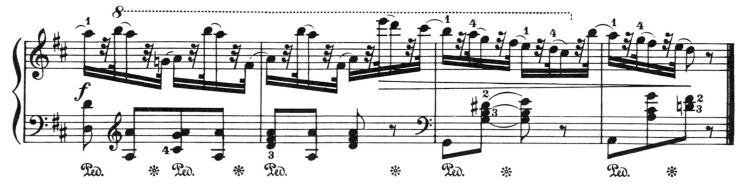

102

F. Chopin. Op. 72, No. 5

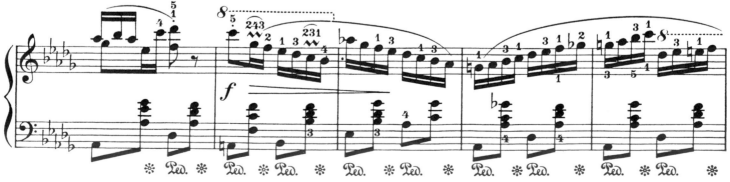

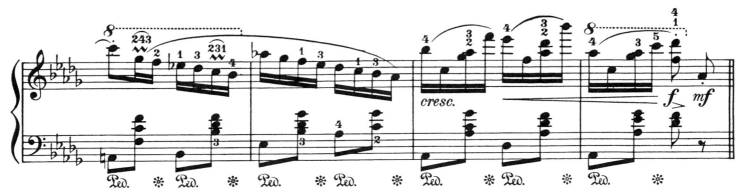

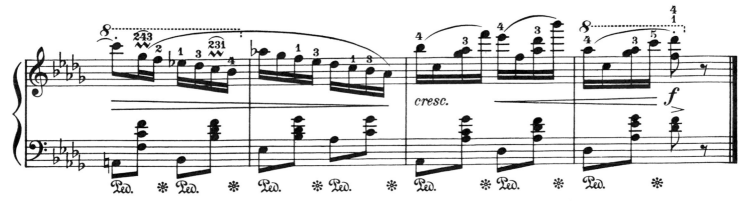